INTRODUCING THE STAR OF THE BOOK

★ COELOPHYSIS ★

(SEE-low-FY-sis)

DID YOU KNOW...

that *Coelophysis* is one of the oldest dinosaurs and one of the best known as thousands of fossils were discovered all in one place. More about that later!

Coelophysis means 'hollow form'

SETTING THE SCENE

It all started around 231 million years ago (mya), when the first dinosaurs appeared, part-way through the Triassic Period.

Coelophysis lived during the late Triassic and early Jurassic periods from 208 – 195 million years ago.

TRIASSIC
←···· lasted 51 million years ····→

JURASSIC
←···· lasted 56 million years ····→

252 million years ago

201 million years ago

The Age of the Dinosaurs had begun, a time when dinosaurs would rule the world!

Scientists call this time the

MESOZOIC ERA

(mez-oh-zoh-ic)

and this era was so long that they divided it into three periods.

CRETACEOUS

lasted 79 million years

145 million years ago   66 million years ago

WEATHER REPORT

The world didn't always look like it does today. At the time when the dinosaurs first appeared, during the late Triassic period, the land was all stuck together in one supercontinent called Pangaea. It stayed that way until the start of the Jurassic Period.

TRIASSIC 220 mya

Named after three distinct rock layers found in Northern Europe

TRIASSIC

Very hot, dry and dusty

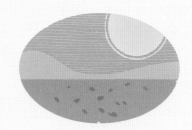

JURASSIC

Hot, humid and tropical

CRETACEOUS

Warm, wet and seasonal

The word Pangaea means 'whole' describing the time when there was only one huge landmass covering nearly a third of the planet's surface

HOMETOWN

Here's what's been discovered so far and where...

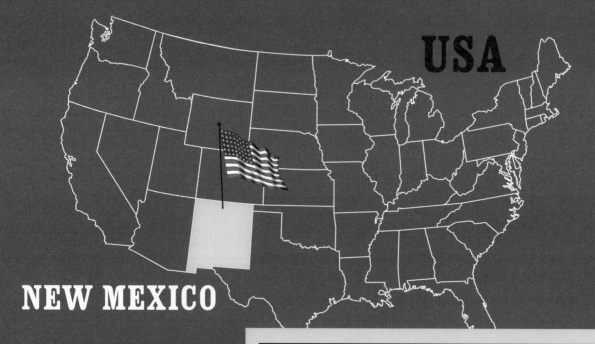

USA

NEW MEXICO

PALAEONTOLOGIST

EDWARD DRINKER COPE

NAMED COELOPHYSIS IN 1889

Thousands of bones, several
hundred complete and near-
complete skeletons

The discovery of thousands of fossils in a bone bed (a collection of
many, many fossils in one place) in 1947 by George Whitaker at Ghost
Ranch, New Mexico, is claimed to be the greatest ever find in North
America of a dinosaur from the Triassic Period.

As adults, juveniles and babies were found together, alongside other
animals, palaeontologists think that that they were travelling in a
large flock and had been buried quickly in a flash flood.

VITAL STATISTICS

Coelophysis, like several of the earliest Triassic dinosaurs, was small and lightly built.

Let's look at *Coelophysis* and see what's special, quirky and downright amazing about this dinosaur!

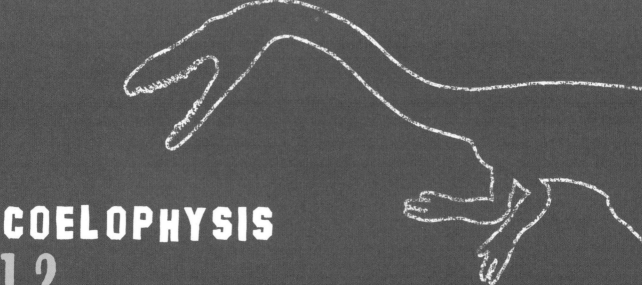

COELOPHYSIS

1.2 m high from toe to hip

hip height
measurement

As so many fossils
have been found,
scientists have
been able to see
the difference
between the males
and females.

DOOR
2 m high

7 YEAR OLD BOY
1.2 m high 25 kg

DAD
1.82 m high

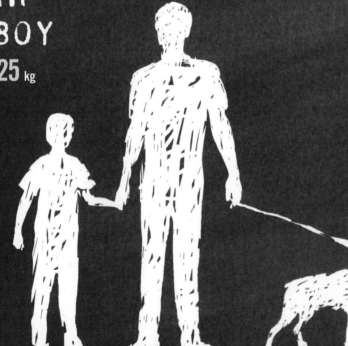

BOXER DOG
0.6 m high 0.6 m long 25 kg

MOUSE

COELOPHYSIS

Length: **up to 3 m**

Height: **1.2 m**

Weight: **25 kg**

SCARY SCALE

How does *Coelophysis* rate?

NOT SCARY

| 1 | 2 | 3 | 4 | 5 |

↑

Low for a carnivore as it
was one of the smallest
predators of its time

ROARRrrrrr!!!

There were very few dinosaurs around to be scared of, but there were lots of other animals that *Coelophysis* had to watch out for. Read on to find out who they were.

| 6 | 7 | 8 | 9 | 10 |

SCARY

A single *Coelophysis* may not have been frightening, but a flock of a hundred or more would have scared plenty of animals!

BRAININESS

When dinosaurs were first discovered
they were thought to be quite stupid!

Then a few scientists thought that some dinosaurs had
a second brain close to their butt! That's now just a myth.

Today scientists know that dinosaurs had one brain and were
intelligent for reptiles. Some were among the most intelligent
creatures alive during the Mesozoic Era, although
still not as smart as most modern mammals.

By looking at the:

Body size

Size
of the
brain

Sense
of
smell

Eyesight

Scientists can tell how they rated against each other...

WHERE DOES COELOPHYSIS, A MEAT-EATING DINOSAUR, STAND ON THE 'BRAINY SCALE'?

TROODON
(TRU-oh-don)

$^{10}/_{10}$
CARNIVORE

COELOPHYSIS
(SEE-lo-FY-sis)

$^9/_{10}$
CARNIVORE

ALLOSAURUS
(AL-oh-SAW-russ)

$^8/_{10}$
CARNIVORE

IGUANODON
(ig-WAHN-oh-DON)

$^6/_{10}$
HERBIVORE

STEGOSAURUS
(STEG-oh-SAW-russ)

$^4/_{10}$
HERBIVORE

DIPLODOCUS
(DIP-lod-oh-CUSS)

$^2/_{10}$
HERBIVORE

These dinosaurs are drawn to
scale in relation to each other!

SPEED-O-METER

S L O W

① ② ③ ④ ⑤

Coelophysis was a light, speedy meat-eating bipedal dinosaur and had great eyesight. The perfect combination to help it hunt down prey and escape from predators.

6 7 8 9 10

F A S T

SPECIAL BITS

As one of the first, successful meat-eating dinosaurs, *Coelophysis* was quite small compared to the giants that were still to come!

Dinosaurs had evolved into various shapes and sizes by the end of the Triassic Period, but it would not be until the next period of time when they would rule the world!

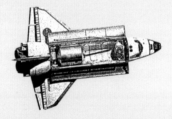

that a *Coelophysis* fossil was taken into space! On January 22, 1998, a skull travelled on board the Space Shuttle Endeavour and was taken to the Russian MIR Space Station! How cool is that?

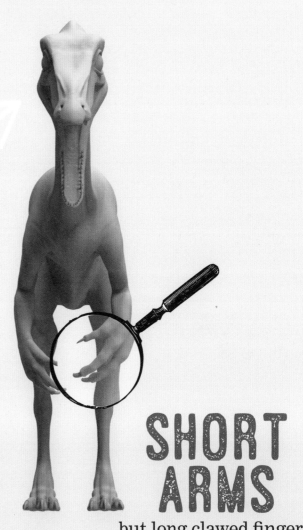

LONG TAIL
to help steer whilst running fast

SKULL
long, shallow skull

BIPEDAL
means that the animal walked on two legs. Dinosaurs' legs were positioned directly underneath their bodies, like mammals, which makes them different from crocodiles and lizards which have legs that stick out from the side of their bodies.

SHORT ARMS
but long clawed fingers, to help grasp its food

TEETH

You can tell a lot about a dinosaur just by looking at its teeth. Let's look at what kind of teeth *Coelophysis* had and what food it ate.

Coelophysis had a mouth packed full of small, recurved (pointing backwards) teeth, that were serrated on the front and back, making them perfect for slicing through flesh.

Here's an interesting fact, most snakes have recurved teeth too.

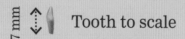 Tooth to scale

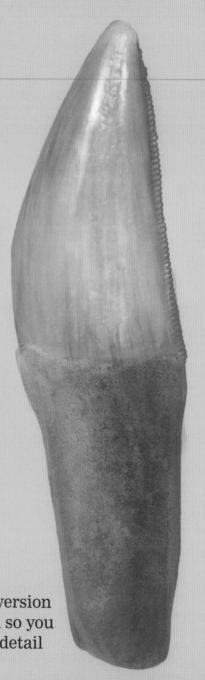

Over-sized version of the tooth so you can see the detail

DIET

Coelophysis was a carnivore, which means that it wasn't interested in eating plants! Studies suggest it probably preyed on small lizard-like animals, small crocodilians and fish. As lots and lots of skeletons have been found together, scientists think that they may have hunted in packs, so might have chased larger prey together.

In the past, *Coelophysis* was falsely accused of being a cannibal (an animal that eats the flesh of its own kind)! Some specimens of *Coelophysis* found at Ghost Ranch appeared to have the remains of babies preserved in their stomach contents, BUT it turned out that these remains belonged to small reptiles instead.

REDONDASAURUS (RE-don-dah-SAW-russ)

Even though dinosaurs were not the dominant animals in the late Triassic period, *Coelophysis* had to watch out for other, bigger predators, like the crocodile-like phytosaurs.

Redondasaurus was a large phytosaur with a very large snout with big teeth. It would probably lurk close to the water's edge, waiting for a *Coelophysis* to come fishing!

WHO LIVED IN THE SAME
NEIGHBOURHOOD?

POSTOSUCHUS

(POST-oh-SOOK-uss)

No, not a dinosaur or a crocodile! This was one of the apex (top of the food chain) predators of the late Triassic period and was very big and very frightening!

Postosuchus was much larger than *Coelophysis* and bones have been found in the same environment which suggests that it probably preyed on *Coelophysis*!

WHICH ANIMAL ALIVE TODAY IS MOST LIKE COELOPHYSIS?

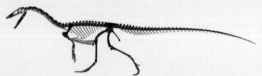

With so many skeletons found at Ghost Ranch, ranging from babies to adults, palaeontologists have learned a lot about the body of *Coelophysis*. It looked a little like large flightless birds that are alive today, such as the emu.

Both have long, slender legs and long necks.

The female emu is larger than the male and that might have been the same for *Coelophysis*. Both males and females have been identified from the many skeletons at Ghost Ranch.

The males are robust, shorter and stockier with a short skull and short neck, whereas the females are longer, slender and have a long skull and long neck. Differences between males and females have even been identified in baby *Coelophysis* too!

WHAT'S SO SPECIAL ABOUT COELOPHYSIS?

WHEN COELOPHYSIS LIVED

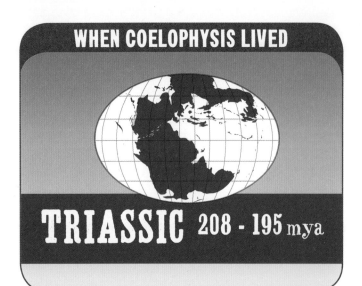

TRIASSIC 208 - 195 mya

TOOTH SIZE

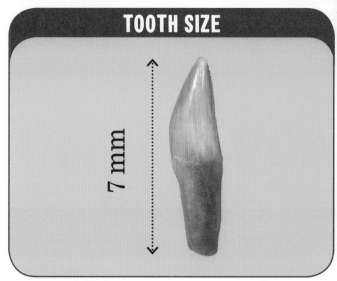

7 mm

WEIGHT

25 KG

FAST OR SLOW?

SPEED

out of 10

8

THE BEST BITS!

DISCOVERED, SO FAR

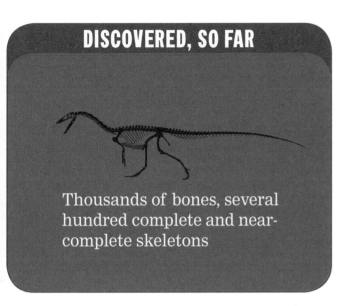

Thousands of bones, several hundred complete and near-complete skeletons

HOW FRIGHTENING?

SCARY

4
on its own

7
in a group

MEAT OR PLANTS?

MEAT

SPECIAL BITS

LONG CLAWS

LONG TAIL

WHAT'S NEXT ?

OTHER EXCITING TITLES AVAILABLE NOW!

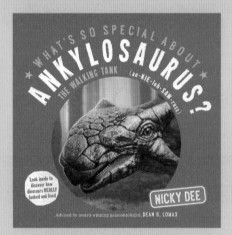

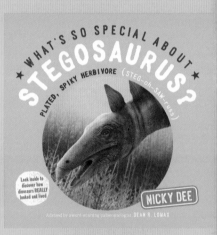

ANKYLOSAURUS
the walking tank

T. REX
the 'King of the Dinosaurs', the ultimate bone cruncher

STEGOSAURUS
plated, spiky herbivore

COMING SOON

Megalosaurus
the very first dinosaur to be named

Triceratops
horned and frilled with a massive skull

Diplodocus
long necked, whip-tailed giant

Leaellynasaura
tiny, bug-eyed, long tailed Australian

Join the 'What's So Special Club'

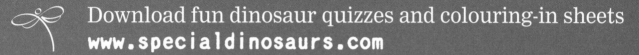

JOIN OUR FREE CLUB

Download fun dinosaur quizzes and colouring-in sheets
www.specialdinosaurs.com

Enter the exciting world of a 3D artist and discover how a 3D dinosaur is created and made to look real!

Find out more about our experts and when they first became fascinated by dinosaurs.

Who is Nicky Dee? Meet the author online.

Join the club and be the first to hear about exciting new books, activities and games.

Club members will be first in line to order new books in the series!

Copyright Published in 2016
by The Dragonfly Group Ltd

email info@specialdinosaurs.com
website www.specialdinosaurs.com

First printed in 2016
Copyright © Nicky Dee 2016
Nicky Dee has asserted her right under the
Copyright, Designs, and Patents Act 1988 to be
identified as the Author of this work.

ISBN: 978-0-9935293-3-7

Printed in China

ACKNOWLEDGEMENTS

Dean R. Lomax
talented, multiple award-winning
palaeontologist, author and science
communicator and the consultant
for the series.
www.deanrlomax.co.uk

David Eldridge
specialist book designer

Gary Hanna
thoroughly talented 3D artist

Scott Hartman
skeletons and silhouettes, professional
palaeoartist and palaeontologist

Ian Durneen
skilled digital sketch artist of the
guest dinosaurs

Ron Blakey
Colorado Plateau Geosystems Inc.
creator of the original
paleogeographic maps

My family
patient, encouraging and wonderfully
supportive. Thank you!

To find out more about our artists, designers
and illustrators please visit the website
www.specialdinosaurs.com